_____

and

_____

_____

Honeymoon Location

Dates: _____

Best wishes on this wonderful journey as
you build your new lives together.

Love is not finding a perfect
person; it's finding a person
perfect for you.

There is no remedy for love
but to love more.

- Thoreau

The first to apologize is the
bravest. The first to forgive is
the strongest. And the first to
forget is the happiest.

Success in marriage does not
come by finding the best person
but by being the best person.

Marriages thrive when each
partner understands that
they are on the same team.

Express Gratitude Daily.

True love may start a beautiful marriage, but it is true friendship that sustains it.

Never start a fight with your
spouse when they're cleaning.

To love is to wish for the
good of the other.

- Thomas Aquinas

Duty makes us do things well, but love makes us do them beautifully.

- Phillips Brooks

Vow to never keep score; even
if you are totally winning.

The madness of love is the
greatest of heaven's blessings.

- Plato

If you tell the truth you don't have to remember anything.

- Mark Twain

When you're wrong, admit it.
When you're right, be quiet.

Made in the USA
Middletown, DE
03 November 2019